DEDICATION

These poems reveal the fluctuation of emotions in various moments of my life. Those variations divulge deep hidden feelings.

I dedicate this book to two special people in my life. The first being my very best friend, more like a sister. Deborah R. Watson passed away in the fall of 1987, she was my soul mate in sisterhood. The second person being my husband Maxwell "Bingo" Cole. I met him in the spring of 1988. Our relationship started with love at first sight, he is my forever love.

CHAPTERS

1. **LOSS AND FOUND**
2. **FEELINGS**
3. **FACES**
4. **LOVE'N**
5. **HIM & ME**
6. **SPIRITUALITY**

CHAPTER 1
LOSS AND FOUND

Page 4. - Grief

Page 5. – Time

Page 6 – Existing

Page 7 – The Past

Page 8 – The Future

GRIEF

IT IS WRITTEN THAT WE WALK THIS LAND ON TIME WE BORROW. AS THAT TIME COMES TO AN END IT DEFINITELY WILL BRING SORROW. THE ANGUISH OF KNOWING MY LOVED ONES WILL MOVE ON AND UP THROUGH THESE YEARS AT TIMES HAS ME CRYING LEAVING MY FACE DRENCHED WITH TEARS. THE WINDING ROAD OF LOST LEADS TO A DEAD END OF HEARTACHE. BEING IN SECLUSION BRINGS ON DISCOURAGING EMOTIONS, I AM BREAVED AND THE LAMENTATION IS OVERWHELMING AS I GRIEVE. THIS WOE THIS GRIEF! WILL BE CARRIED WITHIN MY SOUL FOREVERMORE WITH SELDOM RELIEF.

TIME

IT SEEMS LIKE AN INFINITY HAS PASSED SINCE YOU TRANSCENDED INTO THE LAND OF OUR ANCESTORS, THREE DECADES THAT I HAVE NOT SET EYES ON YOUR FACE OR HAD THE PLEASURE OF YOUR SMILE WARMING MY SOUL. IT BEGAN A NEW ERA IN THIS SISTERLESS PERIOD OF MY EXISTENCE. I WANDERED THROUGH THE DESOLATE UGLY SPACES OF MY HEART AND MIND PLACES WHERE UNDERSTANDING, ASSURANCE, SAFETY AND LOVE USE TO LIE. AS THE HOURS ON THE CLOCK TICKTCKED AWAY CHANGING NORMAL TIME INTO A MAKE BELIEVE WORLD WHERE EVERY SECOND WITHOUT YOU TURNED INTO AN ETERNITY OF HEARTACHE, LOSS, AND DREAD. FROM MOMENT TO MOMENT NOT EVEN THE DESIRE TO CRAWL OUT OF BED. THERE WAS A HOLE LEFT IN ME BY YOUR PHYSICAL DISAPPEARANCE, WHEN YOU WERE TAKEN TO BE IN YOUR GLORY TORE MY HEART AND SOUL APART CHANGING MY LIFE'S STORY.

EXISTING

DAY IN AND DAY OUT MY MIND WANDERS THERE AND ABOUT, SENDING FLASHES OF MEMORIES BEFORE AND YET TO COME THIS MIGHT SOUND FUNNY OR IMPOSSIBLE TO SOME? EYES CLOSED BREATHING MAYBE, MAYBE NOT. KEEPING THAT HEART BEATING COULD SEEM LIKE A LOT RESISTING DAY IN, DAY OUT LIVING AND EXISTING.

THE PAST

A SOLEMN MEMORY THAT HURTS YOUR CORE MUCH LIKE A STOMACH ACHE AFTER TOO MUCH EXERCISE IT'S ALWAYS OFF IN THE DISTANCE NOT TO YOUR SURPRISE. IT'S TIED TO YOUR HISTORY AND GROWS WITH YOU AS YOU GROW INTO YOUR ANTQUITY ALTHOUGH IT'S A MEMOIR OUT OF YOUR BOOK OF LIFE AND SHOULD BE BYGONE, TEARS STILL COME TO YOUR EYES WITH EVERY DETAILED REMEMBRANCE OF A DAY IN THE PAST THAT CAN'T BE FORGOTTEN CAN'T BE LET GO AN AWFUL MEMORY FROM LONG AGO.

THE FUTURE

WHAT IS MY DESTINY MY HOPES AND DREAMS? WHEN I CLOSE MY EYES AND LET MY MIND FLY FREE, REFLECTIONS OF MY FUTURE IS WHAT I FORESEE. SO MANY OPPORTUNITIES FLOAT THROUGH THE AIR AT A RAPID PACE; WILL ANY TAKE ROOT AND PLANT ME IN MY FATE? MY MOTHER SAW MY POTENTIAL MY FATHER SAW WASTE. I SEE IMMINENT WONDERS SO FAR YET SO CLOSE IN FRONT OF ME GOD ONLY KNOWS WHAT HE SET OUT FOR MY LIFE. IT'S LIKE A PROPHESY.

CHAPTER 2

FEELINGS

Page 10. - Solitude

Page 11. – Raining

Page 12. – Waterfall of Emotions

Page 13. – Night Time

Page 14. – Appreciation

SOLITUDE

SURROUNDED YET ALONE FEELING OF BREATHLESSNESS BECOMES OVERWHELMING. I'M HERE BUT IN THE ISOLATION OF MY TWILIGHT MIND; IT'S AN ILLUSION IN THE REMOTE CORNERS OF MYSELF. I TRY PULLING OUT OF THIS TRIBULATION INDUCED SECLUSION, BUT THE SORROWFUL EMOTIONS OVERCOME ME AND MAKE ME OVERLY PRIVATE BUT IT'S ONLY A DELUSION. SLOWLY BECOMING A MIND HERMIT NOT ALLOWING THE SUN TO SHINE. I JUST DON'T PERMIT IT WITHDRAWN AN INTROVERT THE CONVERSATIONS BECOME MUTED, PARTIES EVEN SMALL DINNERS ARE ALL SLOWLY REFUSED MENTALLY BECOMING A RECLUSE WALKING AMONGST THE MULTITUDE FEELING IN COMPLETE SOLITUDE.

RAINING

I HEAR THE RAIN GENTLY FALLING OUTSIDE ON MY BEDROOM WINDOW PANE DRIP DRIP DROP IS THE SOUND THE WATER MAKES AS IT FALLS FROM ROOFTOP AS I LAY IN THE DARK BESIDE THE WINDOW FEELING THE AIR BLOW ON MY FACE.

THE FEELING OF THE COOL BREEZE INFUSED WITH DROPLETS OF RAIN MAKES ME FORGET ALL TIME I'M FLOATING IN SPACE. SOMEWHERE IN THE TWILIGHT VISIONS DANCE IN MY MIND THERE IS NO PAST, NO FUTURE, NO REASON TO FAST FORWARD AND NO REASON TO REWIND. IT'S AS IF THE RAIN AND I HAVE COMBINED. THE COMBINATION MADE ME FLUID ABLE TO CLEANSE MYSELF BECOMING MORE LUCID. AS THE RAIN BEGINS TO SLACK, THE DROPLETS BEGIN TO DRY AND SO DO THE FEARS IN ME. THE RAIN IS SETTING ME FREE.

WATERFALLS OF EMOTIONS

The starting point is always from the top sadness, happiness, elation, and depression can cascade right through you and rapids of changing emotions can make you kind of blue. Voices roaring in your brain breaking down your mainframe. When you close your eyes to find silence in the dark and trace the waves of multiple possibilities so you begin to focus on personal abilities while secretly swimming a pool of despair. Splashes of light break through brining you back here. You spread love in the air so it can cover you everywhere. The power of love is the strongest of all, it can even take control of an emotional waterfall.

__Night Time__

When there's a moonless night and the darkness inches its way in invading your comfort zone, sending your thoughts into the unknown. Thoughts turn into memories lead to sleeplessness. You lay there in the dim flicker of a shining star then shades of memories of who you once were and who you now are. Shadows of people that have come into and out of your life leaving their essence like building blocks forming what you now are.

APPRECIATION

In regard to the light, the light that shines through is a reflection of the favor that comes from in you, while walking with a cloak of esteem draped in reassurance which has eyes looking through glasses of reverence and hands holding plates filled with gratitude. Bitterness changing into sweet food altering of the mind's thinking becoming thankful for having a day's memories tranquil. Kindness being a tribute to one's selflessness and feelings floating on clouds of admiration opening up at your feet into a rainbow of appreciation.

Chapter 3
FACES

Page 16 -VISIONS

Page 17 -THE MASK

Page 18 -IMPERFECTION

Page 19- IMAGINATION

VISIONS

The eyes may be windows to one's soul, but our minds hold the visions of our future while simultaneously taking a glimpse into our past. As a child our daydreams are filled with fun and fancies of ourselves prancing around into the favorite spaces of our vivid imagination. In our aging our frivolous musings gives us the perception that life can change and anything can be done with a clear insight dissecting changes in our own self manifestations one by one. Yes we have the foresight to better the world brining creative visions from our youth to light. Brining tangible dreams to be in a realistic existence is just pure brilliance.

THE MASK

Happy, happy smile, smile it's all just a mask hiding sorrowful things in a present state made by a not so distant past. Questions lingering in the air no one bothers to ask. You want the world to stop you wonder how long will these feelings last? Shades and shadows coming out of the daytime following you haunting you not scared of the light which keeps you feeling in a perpetual state of a moonless night. What's on the outside shows no glimpses of an unstable mind though hidden, the mind still unwinds. You're always looking for something that has not been found and the clock is still ticking into a countdown what is it? Hasn't it been in front of your face what are you expecting from this life's race? Take off the mask reveal the hidden sorrow let go of all bitterness, fears, and hate before the clock stops! Then it will be too late.

THE IMPERFECTION

Self-image full of imperfections seeing every flaw that pops out looking in the mirror wondering who is this starring from the other side. You turn away feeling less beautiful feeling like a fool. Is this crown tilting am I foible? Wanting to believe that it is all part of your uniqueness, or is it a short coming? Needing to feel accepted and not rejected. Nature didn't cause this image to be a defect the lack of nurture did, and lack of kindness has left your views marred try to remember you are wonderfully made and a blessing from God.

THE IMAGINATION

I was told very young my vivid and wild imagination would wrap around my neck with age leading to strangulation but this was not true. The scenes that danced in my head were fantastic as I grew. When real life things left me bored and lonely or life became frustrating imagination cleared my mind those visions where so stimulating I could take such ordinary events and with very little effort mentally I transformed them into almost a fairytale world of my own originality The ability to transmute negative images leaving footprints through a child's mind leading to a beautiful picture is an artistry, it didn't take my life Imagination did not destroy me.

CHAPTER 4
LOVE'N

Page 21- FIRST LOVE

Page 22- SMILES

Page 23- YOU

Page 24- LOVE THROUGH THE LOOKING GLASS

FIRST LOVE

In his warm eyes and caring glare I saw straight to his heart. When he touched me with tenderness and love I relish in the thought of having him with me from now on. Now that we have found each other there is a passion in my soul that has started flame a yearning that I can't explain this youthful stage to know life and love for the first time has me cherishing my thoughts. The feelings I'm having I pray they will never go away, Never leave my mind, Never let me go like a fairy tale with a happy ending. The enchantment a wonderful love spell has come over me my first love.

SMILES

That twinkle in your eyes so bright would bring anyone amusement and delight. Your laugh is contagious, that dimple in your cheek is outrageous. Oh how your grin is like a sunbeam, I might have to shade my eyes from the gleam. Pleasant visions in my mind just the sight of you can make any frown turn upside down. I would run a marathon of miles just to keep you with continuous smiles.

YOU

You bring smiles to my face you fill up what use to be an empty space. You never knew you were placed on this earth to be in my life with me as your wife. The love between us is so strong you are my everything, You chose me and I chose you from the very start, and You'll always hold a special place in my heart. You'll never really know what your love does for me it seems so funny because this love is not new, but believe me when I say my love is unbreakable now, always, and forever simply because you're you.

LOVE THROUGH THE LOOKING GLASS

With every sunrise I look forward to looking into your beautiful eyes. Just looking at you my love brings a calming spirit to my soul, when the outside world is being awful. Your touch and the feel of your warm embrace can bring my racing heart to a steady pace. I smile when you smile and no words need to be spoken, We have that bond that can't be broken. As our love grows and we share this life nothing becomes impossible, I believe our dreams will take flight. You are my fairytale my King, top grade, first class THIS is what I see when looking at you with love through the looking Glass.

CHAPTER 5

HIM ~ N~ ME

Page 26- MARRIAGE

Page 27- ZEN

Page 28- UNCONDITIONALLY

Page 29- JOY

MARRIAGE

The road begins as vows are exchanged leading to a permanent bond getting its start with five simple words "till death do us part" The road whines and curves sometimes up, sometimes down. Up pops a hill or a mound, people choose to climb or just stand and kick dirt around. The wind blows dirt and it gets into their eyes causing them to get lost along the roadside. Obstacles show up people make mistakes and can't deal so they think the fake is real. Soon the wind dies down people's views become clear the barriers get pushed away people freely walk along the roadway with no fear. Marriage who knows where the road will lead when it starts? I believe it leads to the love in one's heart.

<u>Zen</u>

That feeling of a soft breath on the back of your neck that sends chills down your spine, those moments together that stay constantly on your mind, those touches that make your heart skip a beat. The tiny kisses that are a special treat taking your consciousness away that's when you're in a place of Zen that's Him.

Unconditionally

Laying in your arms at night feels so good while you're holding me so tight. Running on stepping stones of pain and stress through the years, you are always there wiping away all my tears. Your love for me and my love for you is a combination of God's love for us I believe this to be true. I wish everyone could be loved like you love me. A love that's giving unconditionally.

<u>JOY</u>

Waking up next to the one you love is such a delight such a feeling of glee. Adoring this abundance of love that pours over me. When giving and accepting love without any fear there is such elation you scream shout and cheer. Ecstasy is what you feel just pure bliss that takes over my body with just one kiss.

CHAPTER 6

SPIRITUALITY

Page 31-The Travel

Page 32-Sadness and Happiness

Page 33-Praise

Page 34-Hopes

THE TRAVEL

While sitting at the window
starring into the night wondering
if the future will be gloomy or
bright. Sometimes not knowing
your mind can go crazy and wild,
then changing to calm and mild.
The love in your heart has you
on this unknown expedition.
Suddenly the pressure eases
you begin thinking versus
feeling your mind is in transition.
Your pilgrimage is tedious but
you keep your eye on the prize,
The path you see for yourself
becomes a little clearer in your
eyes. Remembering the order of
your steps though sometimes
hard are always directed by our
Father God.

SADNESS AND HAPPINESS

See with your eyes listen with your ears say no words show no fear. Feeling with your heart and loving from your soul. Creating a happy content life is your goal. God is in the air evil is in the wind blowing confused thoughts everywhere. Speaking lets you breathe the air and exhale the wind but where do you stop? Where do you begin? Your words and thoughts will be blessed and clear, even if you say little to no words and show no fear.

PRAISE

Looking back at my life and remembering all the things I've been through the sun still came out and dried up the rain's dew.
PRAISE HIM

Who can hold me? Who can love me unconditionally? Who will stay in my life permanently?
PRAISE HIM

There is only one in all the world that can take away any pain just call on him say his name. If you ask me tomorrow a week from now or even a year just listen and hear I'll tell you the same, I know his name and I

PRAISE HIM

HOPES

Hopes dreams wishes of one's being. Wanting, needing to be better than before, better than your ancestral past having the expectation of being on a higher plain. Trying to build a legacy with faith Brick by Brick carrying optimism on your back with love and understanding in a sack of belief that you can be. You have to be walking into the anticipation of what will be, leads you to have a deep aspiration that fills your heart with a ferocious ambition.

www.ingramcontent.com/pod-product-compliance
Lightning Source LLC
Chambersburg PA
CBHW070304010526
44108CB00039B/1863